TWELVE KEYS TO PRAYER

Twelve Keys to Prayer

Jerome Kodell, O.S.B.

A Liturgical Press Book

THE LITURGICAL PRESS
Collegeville, Minnesota

Cover design by Nora Koch

1   2   3   4   5   6   7   8

ISBN 0-8146-2580-0

Our age in the Church is marked by a great interest in the nature and methods of prayer. This interest was triggered initially by the return to the sources of our Christian heritage at Vatican Council II. The prayer tradition of the Church has been revealing its amazing riches ever since.

Like rich fare of any kind, too much too fast can produce nausea or, more likely in this case, bewilderment. Some of us have stood before the mountain of information about prayer and wondered where to get a foothold. There is so much material, so many new books, so many voices of experience. How do I sort through it all?

St. John Climacus said many centuries ago that prayer is a natural faculty, like eyesight, built into each person by the Creator. We know instinctively something about the use of our eyes (no instruction is needed to begin seeing); but experienced users can tell us about care of the eyes, and can interpret color and design for us, passing on what they have learned from looking at the world.

So it is with most natural faculties. We can use them, but to develop their use it helps to have a teacher, and for prayer we have the best: the teacher of the art of prayer is God. "The interior ways of prayer are made known to us by God alone, who gives to each the necessary knowledge and bestows the gift of prayer on those who pray" (*Ladder of Divine Ascent,* 28).

The last words of St. John's statement formulate in another way that we cannot learn prayer simply from the instruction of others, whether personally or from books and tapes. God bestows the gift of prayer on those who pray. We learn how to do it by doing it. Early in this century, another revered teacher of prayer, Abbot John Chapman, made this point in a memorable staccato phrase: "The only way to pray is to pray, and the way to pray well is to pray much" (*Spiritual Letters,* 53).

Granted that fundamental truth, it is also true that as we pray we can be tutored in our response to God's love by the helpful hints of graduate students who have sat at God's feet before us. The centuries-long Christian tradition is rich with insights about the life of prayer learned by the saints on the altar of experience. Even if they cannot teach us to pray in the intimacy learned only from God, experienced prayers can share with us some do's and don'ts and some insights they have gleaned during their own journeys.

A Rich Tradition

I have gathered some pointers about prayer handed down from elder brothers and sisters in the Catholic tradition who have gone before us in the sign of faith leaving a legacy of prayer experience. I call them "Twelve Keys to Prayer" but not "The Twelve": these are just some of the many that have been handed down to us, but they are a good start.

1) *Prayer is a relationship.* Prayer can be explained and defined in various ways, but we always return to the realization that prayer is a personal communication between a child of God and God. There are millions of words and ideas to assist us in prayer, from the liturgical rituals to the personal prayer books to the Bible and other books and articles about prayer. And there are rosaries and crucifixes and other images and symbols (sacramentals), all very helpful in our journey of prayer. But all the words and things of prayer must lead to personal communication with God; otherwise they may become subtle substitutes for prayer or even superstitious objects.

God has created each of us personally and uniquely. There are no copies. Neither are any two relationships with God identical. The spiritual life is a voyage of new discovery. If we spend time with God, we are gradually drawn into communion, learning to pray by praying. We can never quite explain it, any more than we can explain other love relationships.

2) *True prayer, like true love, is a decision, not a feeling.* In even the most intimate loving relationships, feelings come and go. Spouses or children or friends inspire us at one moment, nauseate us the next. This may be independent of anything they have done or any change we can detect. To a great extent, our feelings have a mind of their own. What cements a relationship is decision and commitment. We cannot judge the fervor of our prayer by the strength or weakness of our feelings: the coldest day of prayer may really be the warmest. Fervor proves itself in the living out of the commitment.

The making of a commitment may be flooded with powerful feelings. Think of a wedding day, a religious profession, an ordination. In those moments there is no darkness, only light. After that, though, feelings come and go, often leaving us high and dry at critical times. It is precisely in those moments that the promise is an anchor, holding us true to our purpose and carrying us through. Fidelity to prayer is a more reliable guide to spiritual growth than prayer's varying quality from day to day.

3) *Involuntary distractions do not interrupt prayer.* As a decision, prayer is primarily an action of the will, not of the mind. The mind, constantly aggressive for thoughts and ideas, may momentarily take our attention away from the focus of our prayer without breaking the commitment to pray at that moment. The fervor of prayer is not measured by the clarity of the focus, but by the intensity of the desire. An involuntary distraction no more breaks our communication of love with God than the spontaneous thought of their child during a kiss breaks the expression of love between husband and wife.

This means that we may spend a good part of the time set aside for prayer in fighting distractions. As long as we are still fighting, the prayer is uninterrupted because the decision is unbroken. We may end our prayer not really knowing what we have done with our time, though we have intended to pray the whole time, and every attempt at prayer is prayer.

There is satisfaction and a kind of control in knowing what we have done in prayer. If distractions lead us to lay down this control trusting in God's mercy, rather than being an obstacle they will serve as a means to pure prayer.

4) *Prayer is not a matter of thinking but of loving.* To put it in the words of St. Teresa of Avila: "The important thing is not to think much but love much." This statement does little more than throw into relief much of what has already been said. It does contrast prayer and thinking rather than prayer and feeling as in the preceding number. Locating prayer in the will puts us all on an equal footing before God, no matter what our differences in intellectual gifts. We can all love. And the knowledge of love is greater than the knowledge of thought. "No one can fully comprehend the uncreated God by knowledge; but each person, in a different way, can grasp him fully through love" (*The Cloud of Unknowing*, 4).

Thinking about God and the things of God is a very good preparation for prayer, but it is not prayer. The same is true of spiritual reading. Reading about the spiritual life remains preliminary, as does the reflective thinking called meditation, even when the subject is the sacred Scriptures. These practices are excellent background for prayer, but if we let them exhaust our time of prayer, meanwhile failing to move on to direct communication or communion with God, our spiritual progress may slow to a crawl. The mind will fill with ideas until it becomes heavy and bored. Smart is not necessarily holy. Instead, we must move on from holy thoughts to acts of love.

5) *Short times of prayer daily are better than one long time weekly.* This doesn't mean that shorter is better, but is rather

an emphasis on frequency and consistency. Long or short is not the issue. Like any relationship between persons, prayer flourishes by contact. Absence may make the heart grow fonder; or it will make the heart forgetful. As we grow in familiarity with God, it becomes easier to slip into prayer without worrying what we will say or whether we will say anything. Just being in one another's presence is communion.

Awkward silence is a worry when we do not know one another, because it threatens uncertainty or emptiness, "dead silence." Between friends silence does not have to be artificially filled; it is already filled with shared presence. In God's case, this is definitely graced presence. To enter that sphere daily is like going regularly back to the well.

A regular pattern of frequent prayer also makes prayer easier. Contemporary writer Richard Foster has noted: "It is harder to pray inconsistently than consistently in the same way that it is harder to play a good game of tennis when we practice only once in a while."

6) *Public prayer will not make up for private.* Vatican Council II stated the priority of the liturgy in the prayer life of the Church.

"The liturgy is the summit toward which the activity of the Church is directed; at the same time it is the fountain from which all her power flows" (*Constitution on the Sacred Liturgy*, #10). But the Fathers also noted that the full effectiveness of this public prayer depends on the fervor of the individual participants (#11).

This kind of fervor comes from a personal relationship with God established and fostered outside the times of community worship. Without that, an individual's participation goes up or down with the emotions, or settles into a dull boredom.

Sad to say, it is even possible to participate in public worship without faith, perhaps from social pressure or force of habit. The antidote for that is personal prayer, because it is impossible to continue consistent private prayer without faith.

7) *Don't expect the reward of prayer in the time of prayer.* This is for those who are not beginners. For those beginning the spiritual journey, feelings are often intense during the time of personal prayer. This is a dynamic of the "courtship" period, when God is inviting us to a deeper relationship.

The time comes when the warm feelings in prayer are rare or even absent for short or long periods. This is not a sign of God's absence or distance, but is a safeguard to keep us from stalling or stagnating on the way to God. We could mistake the atmosphere of prayer for God if our love and motives did not have this purifying test.

For most faithful prayers there is no rhyme or reason to the dryness or feelings they experience in the time of prayer. They may feel nothing on most days, but if they remain constant in spite of the dryness, they will be surprised by the warmth of God's closeness outside of prayer when they are not expecting it.

8) *The proof of prayer is in the way we treat others.* Some people are naturally attracted to prayer, others are not. Some feel good during prayer, others do not. Some are always distracted, others rarely. Some focus on religious ministries, others on secular jobs. Some perform heroic feats, even miracles, while others plod. Some know theology, others don't. None of this proves anything about the prayer of these various people.

"If I have the gift of prophecy and comprehend all mysteries and all knowledge; if I have all faith so as to move mountains, but do not have love, I am nothing" (1 Cor 13:2). The proof of prayer is Christian love, which means simply wanting and doing what is best for the other and exhibits the virtues listed by Paul further on in the chapter just quoted: "Love is patient, love is kind . . . ."

Faithful prayer will make love grow.

9) *You will stop praying or stop sinning.* This is a maxim of St. Teresa of Avila. It is another way of stating the principle that a house divided against itself cannot stand. One who chooses God will not continue choosing what is not of God.

Because growth in holiness is not discernible on a day to day basis, we think our prayer is ineffective and useless, especially when we feel nothing. This maxim is an encouragement to realize that something is happening. God is working.

If I am faithful to my daily communion with God, sinful habits, tendencies, and attitudes will gradually dissipate and virtues will take their place. I remember a woman seeking spiritual renewal, who after dedicating herself to fifteen minutes of prayer daily for six months, complained that she was a failure because she could never remain concentrated during her time of prayer. On closer examination, we discovered that during this time she had grown significantly in patience, a primary fruit of faithful prayer.

10) *The warmth of spiritual courtship is followed by the cold of spiritual testing.* Here we have a fundamental teaching of the masters of prayer, a formal statement of the principle referred to earlier. St. John of the Cross says that the journey is not for those who have "merely a sweet tooth."

A honeymoon period may come abruptly to an end in an experience of coolness, even coldness. The absolute conviction of an earlier time is suddenly replaced by doubt: Did I really experience God or was it an illusion? Does God even exist? Those embarking on a religious vocation may be tormented by temptations to leave.

The good news is that God is very involved in this "dark night of the spirit," which if borne faithfully can be a time of rapid spiritual growth.

11) *No one with a prayer life says that prayer doesn't work.* Complaints about the effectiveness of prayer come from those who pick and choose at prayer, using it as a means to

deal with crises or passing desires. Of course prayer is disappointing when judged on that basis. The deeper problem is the concept of God as a cash register.

We pray first of all to be with God. From that relationship comes healing—gradual and imperceptible—of the false self with its harmful passions and desires. This results in a change of perspective, what Cardinal Newman calls a new "frame of mind," in which we begin to see things from God's point of view and to rejoice in his presence and love.

Roberta Bondi notes, "If we let prayer be only a means to something we want, it will not be what it can be, and we will not be who we can be."

12) *God is not out there but in here.* Thinking of prayer primarily as a means to personal ends not only limits and narrows our concept of God, it causes us to think of God as separate and distant from ourselves, a supplier in the skies. We pray as if we were sending a fax. But God is present within us. Newman again states: "A true Christian may almost be defined as one who has a ruling sense of God's presence within him." Colossians speaks of "Christ in you, your hope of glory" (1:27).

The more we continue to seek personal communion with God through prayer, the more the awareness of this divine presence grows. The challenges, the pains, the sufferings of life do not change, but because we change, growing in awareness of the loving presence within, life does not oppress us. We are able to find peace in struggles that at an earlier time would have crushed us. In this way, even now, our "sorrow will be turned into joy" (John 16:20).

This presence within, finally, gives us peace about our prayer. We do not have to pray "perfectly"; we just have to pray. The Holy Spirit, God within, does the rest: "The Spirit too comes to the aid of our weakness; for we do not know how to pray as we ought, but the Spirit itself intercedes with inexpressible groanings. And the one who searches hearts knows what is the intention of the Spirit, because it intercedes for the holy ones according to God's will" (Rom 8:26-27).

Selected Bibliography

Bondi, Roberta C. *To Love as God Loves: Conversations with the Early Church.* Philadelphia: Fortress, 1987.

_____. *To Pray and to Love: Conversations on Prayer with the Early Church.* Minneapolis: Fortress, 1991.

Casey, Michael. *The Undivided Heart: The Western Monastic Approach to Contemplative Prayer.* Petersham, Mass.: St. Bede's, 1994.

_____. *Toward God: The Ancient Wisdom of Western Prayer.* Ligouri, Mo.: Triumph, 1996.

Chapman, John. *Spiritual Letters.* London: Sheed and Ward, n.d.

Foster, Richard J. *Prayer: Finding the Heart's True Home.* London: HarperCollins, 1992.

John Climacus, St. *The Ladder of Divine Ascent.* Mahwah, N.J.: Paulist (Classics of Western Spirituality #34), 1982.

John of the Cross, St. *Selected Writings.* Mahwah, N.J.: Paulist (Classics of Western Spirituality #53), 1987.

Johnston, William. *The Cloud of Unknowing.* New York: Doubleday (Image), 1996.

Teresa of Avila, St. *Perfect Love: Meditations, Prayers and Writings.* New York: Doubleday (Image), 1995.